SPOT THE DIFFERENCE

PaRragon

Bath · New York · Singapore · Hong Kong · Cologne · Delhi · Melbourne

First published by Parragon in 2009

Parragon
Queen Street House
4 Queen Street
Bath
BA1 1HE, UK

Design, layout and photo manipulation by

quadrum▪
www.quadrumltd.com

All images © iStock

ISBN: 978-1-4075-8120-0

Printed in Malaysia

Contents

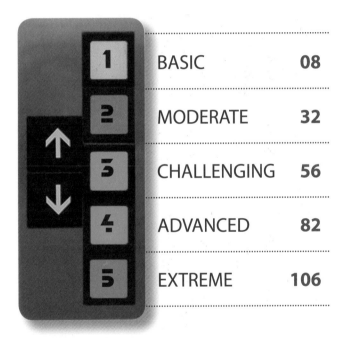

SOLVING THE PUZZLES

1. Give yourself a minute to carefully scrutinise each of the pictures.
2. Then, start comparing them with each other.
3. Each time you spot a difference in a picture, make sure to mark it out.
4. Once you think you are done, cross check your findings with the answers provided at the back of the book.

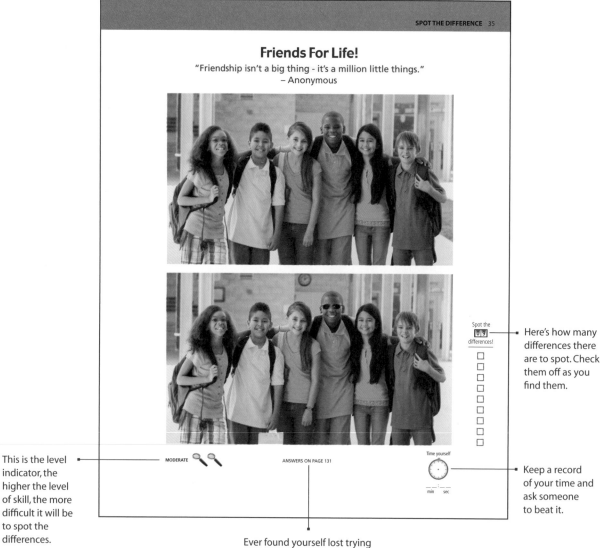

This is the level indicator, the higher the level of skill, the more difficult it will be to spot the differences.

Ever found yourself lost trying to spot a difference? Here's where you can go for help.

Here's how many differences there are to spot. Check them off as you find them.

Keep a record of your time and ask someone to beat it.

1. Take a minute to carefully scrutinise all six images.
2. Five of these pictures are exactly the same. One is just a little different. Can you find the odd one?
3. Don't forget to time yourself!

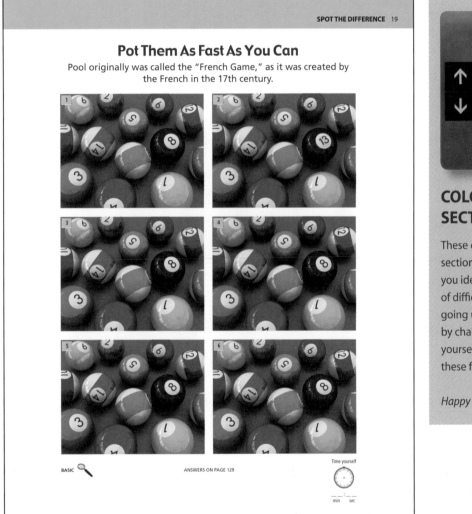

Pot Them As Fast As You Can

Pool originally was called the "French Game," as it was created by the French in the 17th century.

BASIC 🔍   ANSWERS ON PAGE 129

Time yourself

__ __ : __ __
min   sec

5 EXTREME
4 ADVANCED
3 CHALLENGING
2 MODERATE
1 BASIC

COLOR-CODED SECTIONS

These color coded sections will help you identify the level of difficulty. So keep going up the elevator by challenging yourself to master these five levels.

Happy Spotting...

BASIC

Calling all
you rookies
and veterans,
young and
old: Try these
puzzles and see
how good you
actually are.

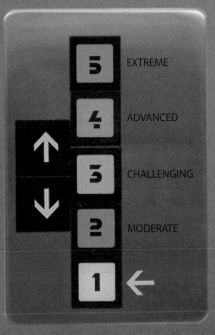

5 EXTREME

4 ADVANCED

3 CHALLENGING

2 MODERATE

1 ←

Eggs–Ellent!

Easter is linked to the Jewish Passover not only for its symbolism but also for its position in the calendar.

BASIC

Spot the
0 9
differences!

☐
☐
☐
☐
☐
☐
☐
☐
☐

BASIC

ANSWERS ON PAGE 128

Time yourself

__ __ : __ __
min   sec

Monkey See, Monkey Do!

"Children have never been very good at listening to their elders, but they have never failed to imitate them." – James Baldwin

Spot the
0 8
differences!

☐
☐
☐
☐
☐
☐
☐
☐

BASIC

ANSWERS ON PAGE 128

Time yourself

__ __ : __ __
min   sec

Spoilt For Choice!

Most Americans claim to own more than 10 t-shirts,
which alone is 1.5 billion t-shirts!

Spot the
0 7
differences!

☐
☐
☐
☐
☐
☐
☐

Time yourself

_ _ : _ _
min   sec

It Don't Matter If It's Black Or White

"Memory is the diary that we all carry about with us." – Oscar Wilde

Spot the
0 7
differences!

☐
☐
☐
☐
☐
☐
☐

 BASIC

ANSWERS ON PAGE 128

Time yourself

__ __ : __ __
min   sec

Bumper To Bumper

Don't drive yourself around the bend trying to find all the differences in these pictures!

Spot the
0 8
differences!

BASIC

ANSWERS ON PAGE 128

Time yourself

_ _ : _ _
min   sec

Patterns In Stone

Did you know that the Moroccan style of architecture is basically an evolution of Berber architecture?

BASIC

Spot the
0 9
differences!

☐
☐
☐
☐
☐
☐
☐
☐
☐

BASIC

ANSWERS ON PAGE 128

Time yourself

__ __ : __ __
min   sec

She Sells, Sea Shells, On The Seashore

Before you start collecting them make sure you find
all the differences.

Spot the
0 6
differences!

☐
☐
☐
☐
☐
☐

BASIC

ANSWERS ON PAGE 129

Time yourself

__ __ : __ __
min   sec

Wanna Play?

"It is better to play than do nothing." – Confucius

Spot the
1 0
differences!

☐
☐
☐
☐
☐
☐
☐
☐
☐
☐

BASIC

ANSWERS ON PAGE 129

Time yourself

__ __ : __ __
min   sec

A Way To A Woman's Heart

Yummy though they look, you can't take a piece till you have found the odd one out!

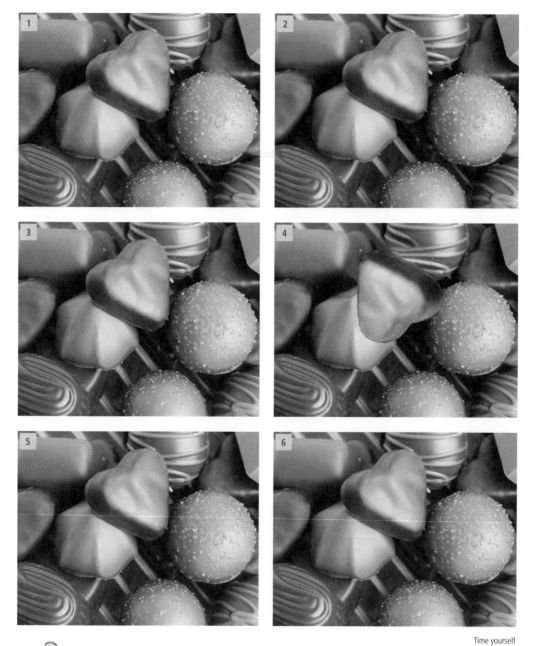

BASIC

ANSWERS ON PAGE 129

Time yourself

__ : __
min   sec

Pot Them As Fast As You Can

Pool originally was called the "French Game", as it was created by the French in the 17th century.

ANSWERS ON PAGE 129

Time yourself

__ __ : __ __
min   sec

What's In A Face?

It takes 43 muscles to frown but only 17 muscles to smile.

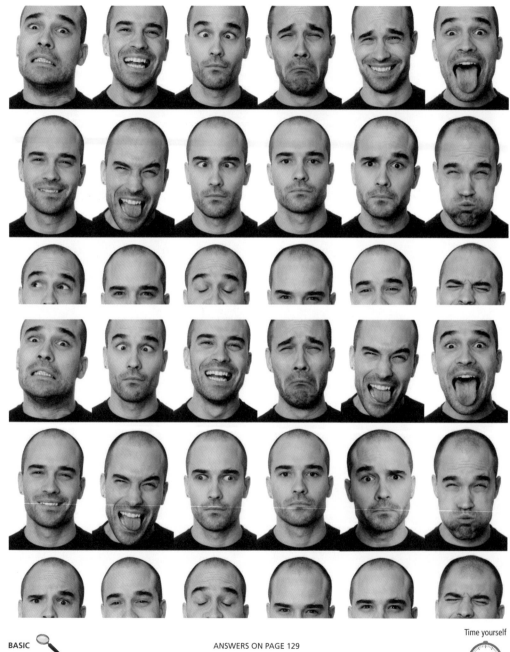

Spot the

0 9

differences!

☐
☐
☐
☐
☐
☐
☐
☐
☐

BASIC

ANSWERS ON PAGE 129

Time yourself

_ _ : _ _
min   sec

Hen Party!

You have a wide range to choose from. But wait a bit…first see if you can spot all the differences.

Spot the
0 8
differences!

ANSWERS ON PAGE 129

Time yourself

___ : ___
min   sec

Piece By Piece

Let's see if you can help the baby by finding the differences in the two images.

Spot the

0 7

differences!

☐
☐
☐
☐
☐
☐
☐

BASIC

ANSWERS ON PAGE 130

Time yourself

__ __ : __ __
min   sec

Room With A View

Before you kick off your shoes and relax, see if you can spot all the differences in the two images.

Spot the
0 7
differences!

☐
☐
☐
☐
☐
☐
☐

BASIC

ANSWERS ON PAGE 130

Time yourself

min   sec

Mine's Much Cooler Than Yours!

Find all the differences in the two images.

BASIC

Spot the
1 0
differences!

☐
☐
☐
☐
☐
☐
☐
☐
☐
☐

BASIC

ANSWERS ON PAGE 130

Time yourself

___ ___ : ___ ___
min   sec

One Block At A Time

Playing with blocks encourages children to make friends and stimulates interaction and imagination.

Spot the
0 6
differences!

☐
☐
☐
☐
☐
☐

Time yourself

__ __ : __ __
min   sec

Home Sweet Home

"It takes hands to build a house, but only hearts can build a home."
– Anonymous

Spot the
0 8
differences!

☐
☐
☐
☐
☐
☐
☐
☐

Time yourself

__ __ : __ __
min   sec

BASIC

ANSWERS ON PAGE 130

Pop Goes The Balloon!

Aren't the balloons bright? Before you choose one, try and spot the odd one out.

BASIC

ANSWERS ON PAGE 130

Time yourself

__ __ : __ __
min   sec

Brushstrokes

There is an odd one amongst the images. See if you can spot it.

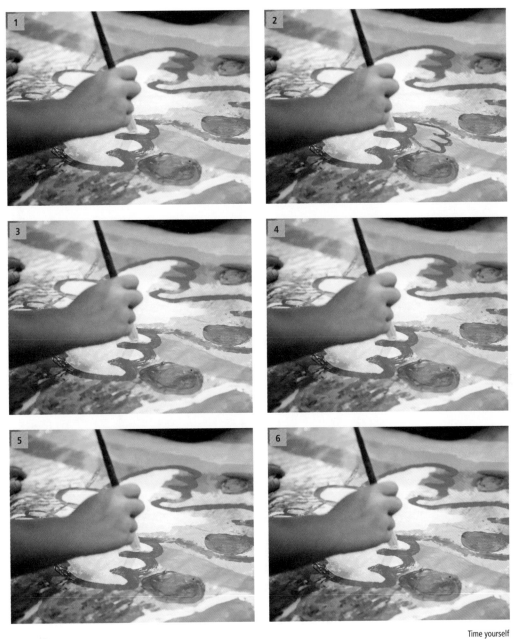

ANSWERS ON PAGE 131

Time yourself

_ _ : _ _
min   sec

Now that you have figured out what to do, try your hand at these slightly tougher puzzles.

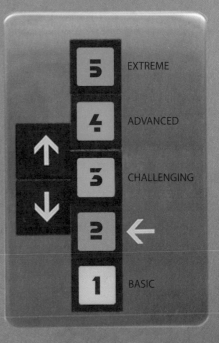

EXTREME

ADVANCED

CHALLENGING

BASIC

Straight Off The Rail!

Sales are so much fun! Before you choose something, see if you can find all the differences.

MODERATE

Spot the
0 7
differences!

Time yourself

__ __ : __ __
min   sec

A Wonderful Wedding Setting!

The tables look so festive, don't they? Take a closer look though as both are not the same.

Spot the
0 7
differences!

☐
☐
☐
☐
☐
☐
☐

MODERATE

ANSWERS ON PAGE 131

Time yourself

_ _ : _ _
min   sec

Friends For Life!

"Friendship isn't a big thing—it's a million little things."
– Anonymous

Spot the
0 9
differences!

☐
☐
☐
☐
☐
☐
☐
☐
☐

MODERATE

ANSWERS ON PAGE 131

Time yourself

__ __ : __ __
min   sec

American Standard Time

See if you can beat the clock and can find all the changes we've made to the images below.

Spot the
0 9
differences!

☐
☐
☐
☐
☐
☐
☐
☐
☐

MODERATE

ANSWERS ON PAGE 131

Time yourself

__ __ : __ __
min   sec

Not Just A Mountain Face!

The nose of each American president on Mount Rushmore is 20 feet long, each mouth 18 feet wide and eyes are 11 feet across.

Spot the
08
differences!

☐
☐
☐
☐
☐
☐
☐
☐

MODERATE

ANSWERS ON PAGE 131

Time yourself

__ __ : __ __
min   sec

A Stitch In Time, Saves Nine

These yarns may look the same, but are not! Look carefully to spot the odd one out.

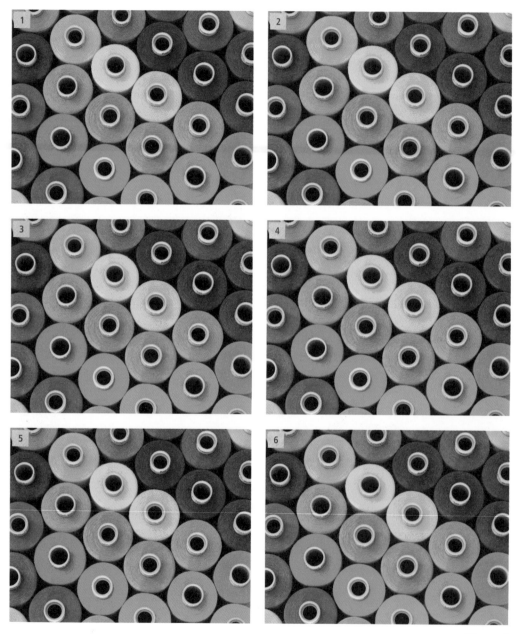

MODERATE

ANSWERS ON PAGE 132

Time yourself

__ __ : __ __
min   sec

Like Mother, Like Daughter

Don't they look happy? Look again though as there is an odd image there.

MODERATE

ANSWERS ON PAGE 132

Time yourself

__ __ : __ __
min   sec

A House For You, A House For Me

Spot the
10
differences!

☐
☐
☐
☐
☐
☐
☐
☐
☐
☐

MODERATE

ANSWERS ON PAGE 132

Time yourself

_ _ : _ _
min   sec

Every Nation's Pride

Did you know that an expert in the history of flags is called a vexillologist?

Spot the
0 9
differences!

☐
☐
☐
☐
☐
☐
☐
☐
☐

MODERATE

ANSWERS ON PAGE 132

Time yourself

__ : __
min   sec

Fitness Is In!

"Fitness—if it came in a bottle, everybody would have a great body."
– Cher

Spot the
0 8
differences!

☐
☐
☐
☐
☐
☐
☐
☐

MODERATE

ANSWERS ON PAGE 132

Time yourself

_ _ : _ _
min   sec

Surf's Up!

Take a break from chasing the waves and look for the changes in the images below.

Spot the
0 9
differences!

MODERATE

ANSWERS ON PAGE 132

Time yourself

___ : ___
min   sec

Standing Tall!

Did you know that the statue of liberty has a 35-foot waistline?

MODERATE

Spot the
0 7
differences!

☐
☐
☐
☐
☐
☐
☐

MODERATE

ANSWERS ON PAGE 133

Time yourself

__ __ : __ __
min   sec

And It's A Goal!

The word "puck" is derived from the Scottish and Gaelic word "puc" meaning to poke, punch, or deliver a blow.

Spot the
0 8
differences!

☐
☐
☐
☐
☐
☐
☐
☐

MODERATE

ANSWERS ON PAGE 133

Time yourself

___ : ___
min   sec

Mirror Images

Did you know that "Snifter" is a British colloquialism for a small amount of liquor in a glass?

Spot the
0 7
differences!

☐
☐
☐
☐
☐
☐
☐

MODERATE

ANSWERS ON PAGE 133

Time yourself

__ __ : __ __
min   sec

The World The Way We See It!

Cheryl Stearns (USA) has held the record for most parachute descents by a woman, with a total of 15,560 jumps, since August 2003.

Spot the
0 8
differences!

☐
☐
☐
☐
☐
☐
☐
☐

MODERATE

ANSWERS ON PAGE 133

Time yourself

__ __ : __ __
min   sec

Dance The Night Away

Before you settle down to watch *Swan Lake,* see if you can spot the differences we have made in the images.

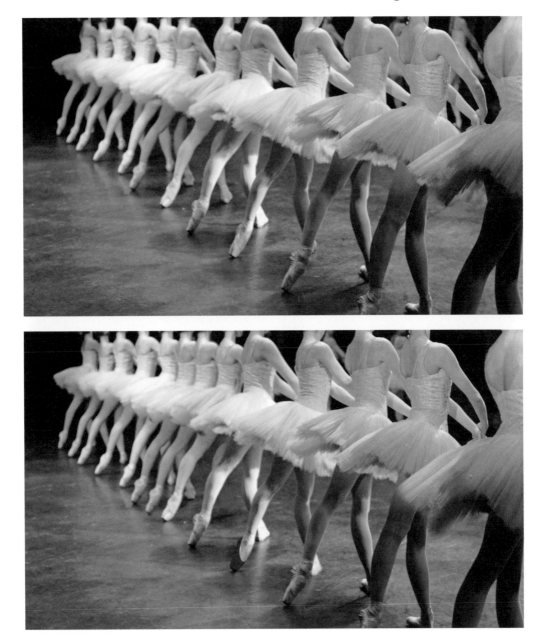

Spot the
0 7
differences!

☐
☐
☐
☐
☐
☐
☐

MODERATE

ANSWERS ON PAGE 133

Time yourself

__ __ : __ __
min   sec

I See Swirls!

Though they look identical, all the swirls are not. Spot the odd one out.

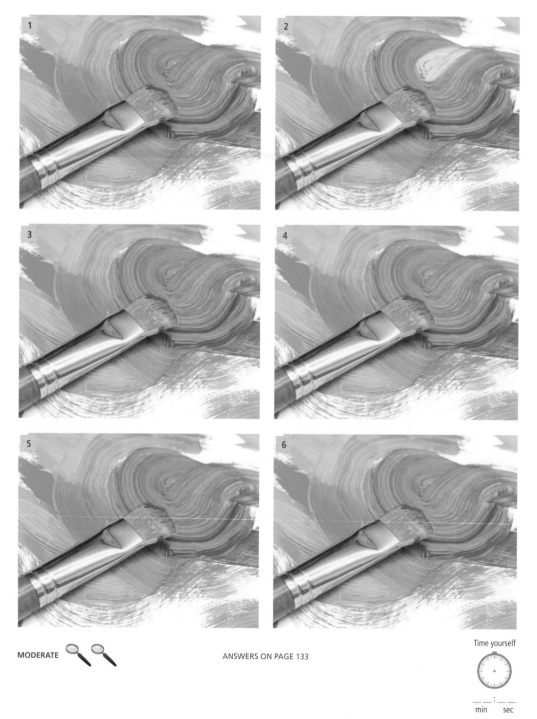

MODERATE

ANSWERS ON PAGE 133

Time yourself

__ __ : __ __
min   sec

Follow The Leader

Can you spot the image that is different?

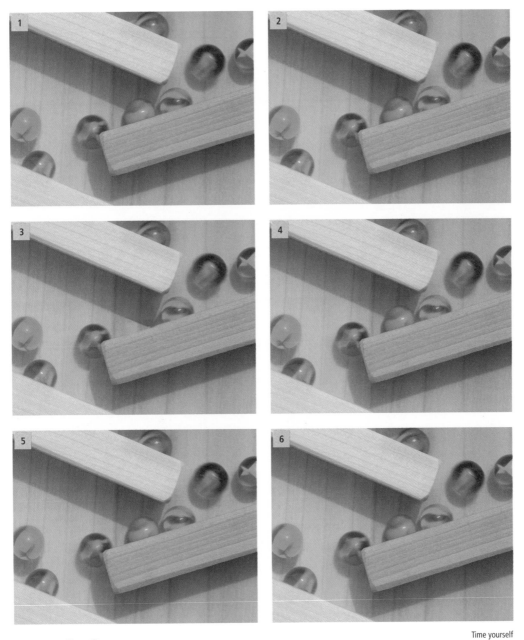

ANSWERS ON PAGE 134

Time yourself

__ __ : __ __
min   sec

Show Me The Way Home!

Though the mazes look identical, we've made some changes. See if you can spot them.

Spot the

0 9

differences!

□
□
□
□
□
□
□
□
□

MODERATE

ANSWERS ON PAGE 134

Time yourself

__ __ : __ __
min   sec

Ready, Set, Go!

"Winning a medal is what every athlete dreams of, and if it is the Olympic gold then that is the icing on the cake." – Jeff Fenech

Spot the
[0][7]
differences!

☐
☐
☐
☐
☐
☐
☐

MODERATE

ANSWERS ON PAGE 134

Time yourself

_ _ : _ _
min   sec

CHALLENGING

Now the going
gets tough!
Time to pit your
brains against
our latest
challenges.

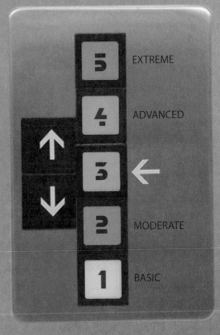

5 EXTREME

4 ADVANCED

3

2 MODERATE

1 BASIC

On Holy Ground

Did you know that the University Church of St Mary's has one of the most beautiful spires in England?

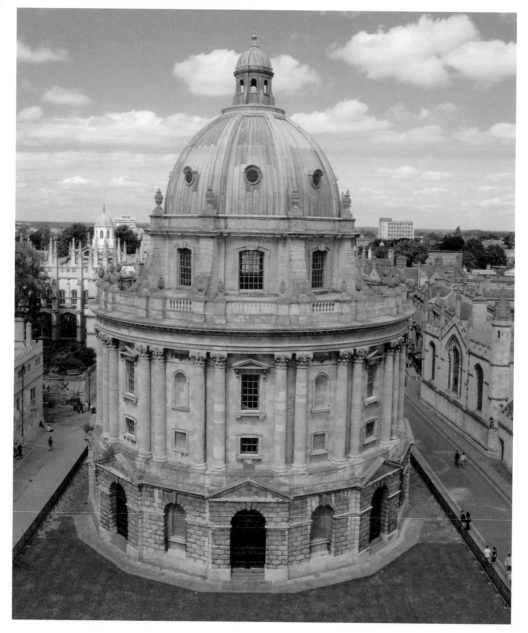

CHALLENGING

Spot the
1 0
differences!

☐
☐
☐
☐
☐
☐
☐
☐
☐
☐

CHALLENGING

ANSWERS ON PAGE 134

Time yourself

__ __ : __ __
min   sec

Van Gogh In The Making!

"Every artist dips his brush in his own soul and paints his own nature into his pictures." – Henry Ward Beecher

Spot the
0 9
differences!

☐
☐
☐
☐
☐
☐
☐
☐
☐

CHALLENGING

ANSWERS ON PAGE 134

Time yourself

__ __ : __ __
min   sec

It's All About The Beiges And Browns

Before you take a picture of this perfect room, see if you can spot the changes in the two images.

Spot the

0 7

differences!

☐
☐
☐
☐
☐
☐
☐

CHALLENGING

ANSWERS ON PAGE 134

Time yourself

__ __ : __ __
min   sec

That's An Ace Of A Serve

A perfectly set table don't you think? Before you pull up your chair, point out the changes in the images.

Spot the
0 6
differences!

☐
☐
☐
☐
☐
☐

CHALLENGING

ANSWERS ON PAGE 135

Time yourself

__ __ : __ __
min   sec

Home Is Where The Heart Is

Fit for an award! However, see if you can spot the changes in the two images.

Spot the
0 7
differences!

☐
☐
☐
☐
☐
☐
☐

CHALLENGING

ANSWERS ON PAGE 135

Time yourself

__ __ : __ __
min   sec

Shining Happy People

There is an odd image here. See if you can spot it.

CHALLENGING   ANSWERS ON PAGE 135

Time yourself

—— : ——
min   sec

Doggone It!

It is said that dogs come from a creature similar to a wolf called Tomarctus. Look closely to find the odd image out.

CHALLENGING

ANSWERS ON PAGE 135

Time yourself

__ __ : __ __
min   sec

You Can Bank On This!

Did you know that the Bank of England has issued banknotes since 1694?

Spot the
0 7
differences!

☐
☐
☐
☐
☐
☐
☐

CHALLENGING

ANSWERS ON PAGE 135

Time yourself

__ __ : __ __
min   sec

It's Mardi Gras Time!

The Mardi Gras celebrations bring in $840 million in revenues for New Orleans alone.

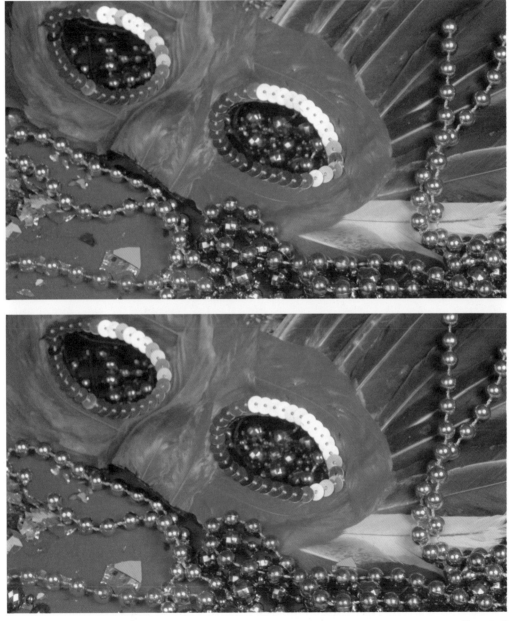

Spot the
0 9
differences!

CHALLENGING

ANSWERS ON PAGE 135

Time yourself

__ __ : __ __
min   sec

Let's have some Salsa

Ready to dig in? Before you do so, see if you spot all the changes
we have made in the images.

CHALLENGING

Spot the
0 9
differences!

☐
☐
☐
☐
☐
☐
☐
☐
☐

CHALLENGING

ANSWERS ON PAGE 136

Time yourself

___ : ___
min   sec

Is That Nemo?

The French grunt can be found in the Western Atlantic from
Bermuda, northern Gulf of Mexico, Caribbean and Brazil.

Spot the
0 8
differences!

☐
☐
☐
☐
☐
☐
☐
☐

CHALLENGING

ANSWERS ON PAGE 136

Time yourself

_ _ : _ _
min   sec

Cash Crunch?

The word "millionaire" was first used by Benjamin Disraeli in his 1826 novel *Vivian Grey*.

Spot the
0 7
differences!

CHALLENGING

ANSWERS ON PAGE 136

Time yourself

_ _ : _ _
min   sec

A Pebble For Your Thoughts!

See if you can spot the differences before you scoop up these pretty pebbles.

Spot the

0 8

differences!

☐
☐
☐
☐
☐
☐
☐
☐

CHALLENGING

ANSWERS ON PAGE 136

Time yourself

__ __ : __ __
min   sec

Shelve That Knowledge!

"Books are not made for furniture, but there is nothing else that so beautifully furnishes a house." – Henry Ward Beecher

Spot the
10
differences!

CHALLENGING

ANSWERS ON PAGE 136

Time yourself

___ : ___
min   sec

A Marvel In Stone

Until the 19th century, Westminster was the third seat of learning in England, after Oxford and Cambridge.

CHALLENGING

Spot the
0 9
differences!

☐
☐
☐
☐
☐
☐
☐
☐
☐

CHALLENGING

ANSWERS ON PAGE 136

Time yourself

__ __ : __ __
min   sec

What A Colorful Joke!
See if you can hold your laughter till you spot
all the differences.

Spot the
10
differences!

☐
☐
☐
☐
☐
☐
☐
☐
☐
☐

CHALLENGING

ANSWERS ON PAGE 137

Time yourself

_ _ : _ _
min   sec

United Colors of Europe

The circle of stars on the Flag of Europe was inspired by the 12-star halo of the Virgin Mary seen in Roman Catholic art.

Spot the
0 7
differences!

Time yourself

min   sec

CHALLENGING

ANSWERS ON PAGE 137

Worth A King's Ransom!

Did you know that the Amber Room in the Charlottenburg Palace has its walls surfaced in decorative amber?

Spot the

0 7

differences!

☐
☐
☐
☐
☐
☐
☐

CHALLENGING

ANSWERS ON PAGE 137

Time yourself

__:__
min   sec

Get 'Em While They're Young!

In at least 25 countries of the world, there is no specified age for compulsory education.

Spot the

1 0

differences!

CHALLENGING

ANSWERS ON PAGE 137

Time yourself

___ : ___
min   sec

Ta Da!

In the 18th century, certain Venetian masks were used to conceal the identity of ladies and gentlemen in gambling houses in Venice.

CHALLENGING

ANSWERS ON PAGE 137

Time yourself

__ __ : __ __
min   sec

Ode To Autumn

"Autumn is a second spring when every leaf is a flower."
– Albert Camus

CHALLENGING

ANSWERS ON PAGE 137

Time yourself

__ : __
min   sec

ADVANCED

Kudos on cracking the earlier puzzles. Now is your chance to raise the bar further.

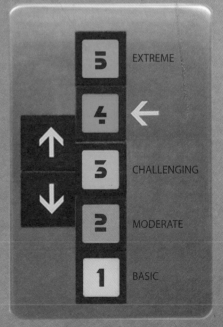

5 EXTREME

4 ←

3 CHALLENGING

2 MODERATE

1 BASIC

Under Construction

Challenging even for Spiderman! See if you can help by spotting the differences.

ADVANCED

Spot the
0 9
differences!

☐
☐
☐
☐
☐
☐
☐
☐
☐

ADVANCED

ANSWERS ON PAGE 138

Time yourself

_ _ : _ _
min   sec

Fearsome Hunter

Did you know that a shark can go without eating for a month?

Spot the
0 7
differences!

☐
☐
☐
☐
☐
☐
☐

ADVANCED

ANSWERS ON PAGE 138

Time yourself

__ __ : __ __
min   sec

May Festivities Are Here Again!

The church of St Andrew in London is named after the maypole that was kept under its eaves and set up each spring till 1517.

Spot the
0 9
differences!

ADVANCED   ANSWERS ON PAGE 138

Time yourself

__ __ : __ __
min   sec

Living In Comfort

"A house is a home when it shelters the body and comforts the soul." – Philip Moffitt

Spot the
1 0
differences!

☐
☐
☐
☐
☐
☐
☐
☐
☐
☐

ADVANCED   ANSWERS ON PAGE 138

Time yourself

__ : __
min   sec

What's Your Current Position?

The early controllers tracked the position of planes using maps and blackboards and little boat-shaped weights called shrimp boats.

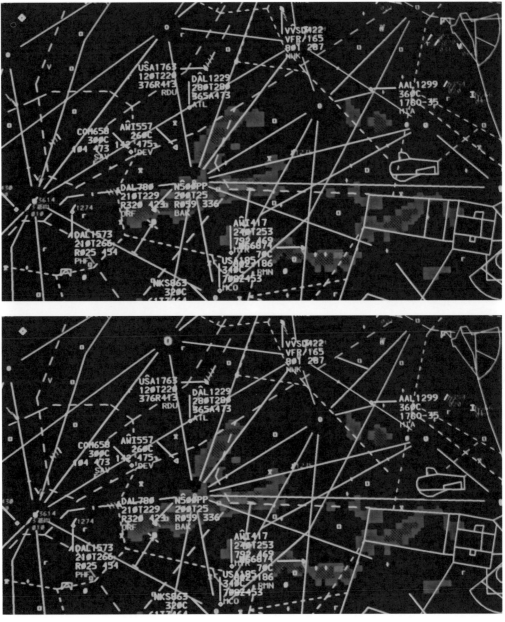

Spot the
0 7
differences!

ADVANCED   ANSWERS ON PAGE 138

Time yourself

___ : ___
min   sec

We Are The Champions!

"If winning isn't everything, why do they keep score?"
– Vince Lombardi

ADVANCED

ANSWERS ON PAGE 138

Time yourself

_ _ : _ _
min   sec

Show Me The Money!

The world's highest denomination note is Hungary 100 Million B-Pengo, issued in 1946.

ADVANCED

ANSWERS ON PAGE 139

Time yourself

___:___
min   sec

Story Time

The first illustrated book for children was published in Germany in 1658.

Spot the
0 8
differences!

☐
☐
☐
☐
☐
☐
☐
☐

ADVANCED   ANSWERS ON PAGE 139

Time yourself

__ __ : __ __
min   sec

Tied Down

Did you know that it is possible to buy a bullet proof tie that will stop a 9mm bullet?

Spot the
0 9
differences!

☐
☐
☐
☐
☐
☐
☐
☐
☐

ADVANCED

ANSWERS ON PAGE 139

Time yourself

__ __ : __ __
min   sec

Perfect Kitchen

A kitchen that any mom will be proud of! But look again, there are changes in the images. See if you can spot them all.

Spot the

differences!

☐ ☐ ☐ ☐ ☐ ☐ ☐ ☐ ☐ ☐ ☐ ☐

ADVANCED

ANSWERS ON PAGE 139

Time yourself

__ __ : __ __
min   sec

Underwater Brilliance

Did you know that coral reefs have existed for more than 200 million years?

Spot the
0 9
differences!

☐
☐
☐
☐
☐
☐
☐
☐
☐

ADVANCED

ANSWERS ON PAGE 139

Time yourself

__ __ : __ __
min   sec

House of Music

The Semperoper is considered to be a prime example of
Dresden-Baroque architecture. How many differences can you find?

ADVANCED

Spot the
0 9
differences!

☐
☐
☐
☐
☐
☐
☐
☐
☐

ADVANCED

ANSWERS ON PAGE 139

Time yourself

__ __ : __ __
min   sec

The Postage Is Paid For!

Did you know that Bhutan once issued a stamp with its national anthem on a playable record?

Spot the

0 8

differences!

☐
☐
☐
☐
☐
☐
☐
☐

ADVANCED

ANSWERS ON PAGE 140

Time yourself

min   sec

Tropical Paradise!

The Hawaiian island of Kauai is home to the wettest spot on Earth.

Spot the
0 9
differences!

ADVANCED

ANSWERS ON PAGE 140

Time yourself

___ : ___
min   sec

Today's Musketeers

"The better part of one's life consists of his friendships."
– Abraham Lincoln

Spot the
0 | **8**
differences!

☐
☐
☐
☐
☐
☐
☐
☐

ADVANCED

ANSWERS ON PAGE 140

Time yourself

__ __ : __ __
min   sec

In The Pink!

Did you know that the eye of a flamingo is larger than its brain?

Spot the
0 7
differences!

☐
☐
☐
☐
☐
☐
☐

ADVANCED

ANSWERS ON PAGE 140

Time yourself

__ __ : __ __
min   sec

Magic Of Wisteria!

Wisteria grows to a height of more than 25 feet and has flower clusters that vary from six inches to a foot in length.

ADVANCED

ANSWERS ON PAGE 140

Time yourself

__ __ : __ __
min   sec

Nations At A Glance!

Nope, all the images are not the same. Spot the odd one out.

ADVANCED

ANSWERS ON PAGE 140

Time yourself

__ __ : __ __
min   sec

Concrete Jungle

Did you know that central London is the headquarters of more than 100 of Europe's 500 largest companies?

Spot the
[0][9]
differences!

☐
☐
☐
☐
☐
☐
☐
☐
☐

ADVANCED

ANSWERS ON PAGE 141

Time yourself

__ __ : __ __
min   sec

Bigger Screen Needed!

In 2004, Paola Antonelli, a curator of architecture and design, included Post-it notes in a show entitled *Humble Masterpieces.*

Spot the
0 | 7
differences!

Time yourself

ADVANCED

ANSWERS ON PAGE 141

EXTREME

Hurray, you're almost a grand master...if you crack a few more, you're the best!

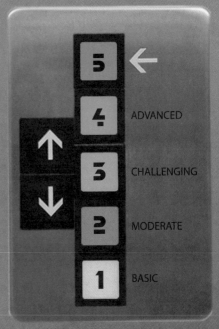

5 ←

4 ADVANCED

↑

↓

3 CHALLENGING

2 MODERATE

1 BASIC

Fine Dining Anyone?

See if you can spot the differences in the otherwise perfect table setting.

EXTREME

Spot the
1 0
differences!

EXTREME

ANSWERS ON PAGE 141

Time yourself

___ : ___
min   sec

Help Needed

Help her sort out all her things. And while you are at it, see if you can also spot the differences.

Spot the
`0` `9`
differences!

☐
☐
☐
☐
☐
☐
☐
☐
☐

EXTREME 🔍 🔍 🔍 🔍 🔍   ANSWERS ON PAGE 141

Time yourself

___ ___ : ___ ___
min   sec

To The Manor Born

Did you know that England, during the period following the Norman Conquest, had more than nine thousand of these manorial estates?

Spot the
1 0
differences!

EXTREME

ANSWERS ON PAGE 141

Time yourself

__ __ : __ __
min   sec

Here's To Us!

During Prohibition in the USA, cocktails were still drunk illegally in establishments known as speakeasies.

Spot the

differences!

☐
☐
☐
☐
☐
☐
☐
☐
☐
☐

EXTREME

ANSWERS ON PAGE 141

Time yourself

__ __ : __ __
min   sec

Snapshots Of A City

Before you sit back and enjoy the setting sun, see if you can spot the differences in the two images.

Spot the
0 8
differences!

EXTREME

ANSWERS ON PAGE 142

Time yourself

_ _ : _ _
min   sec

He Doesn't Look A Day Over Hundred

Did you know that turtles live on every continent except Antarctica?
Spot the odd turtle out from the rest.

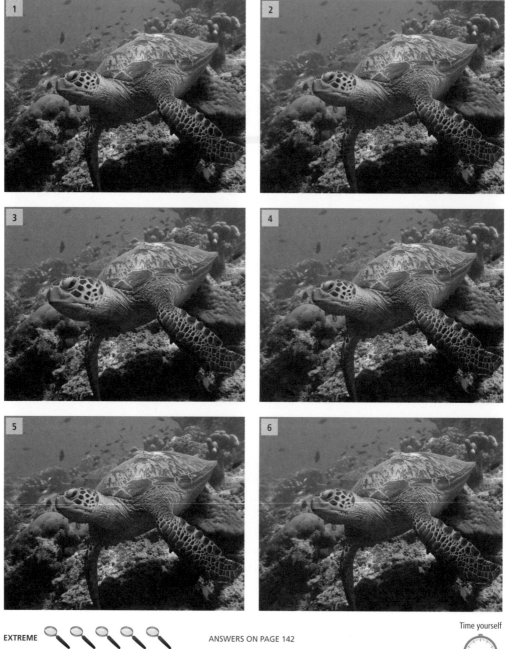

EXTREME

ANSWERS ON PAGE 142

Time yourself

_ _ : _ _
min   sec

One Too Many

It is said that when you spot a bargain, chemicals that create feelings of well-being are released into the brain making you happy.

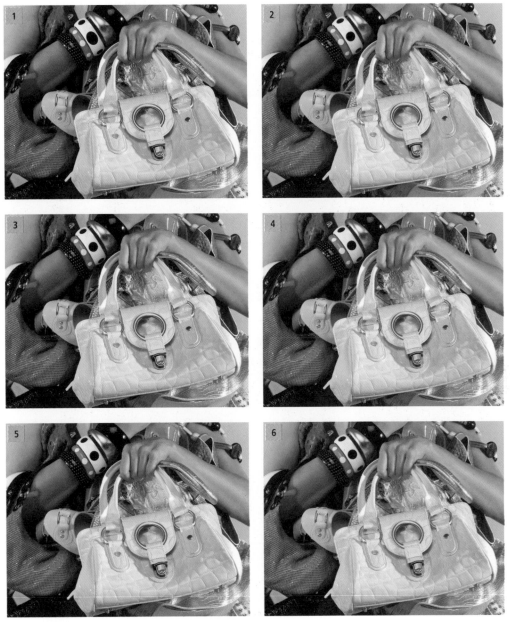

EXTREME

ANSWERS ON PAGE 142

Time yourself

__ __ : __ __
min   sec

Melodies Unlimited!

"Music washes away from the soul the dust of everyday life."
– Berthold Auerbach

Spot the
1 0
differences!

EXTREME

ANSWERS ON PAGE 142

Time yourself

__ __ : __ __
min   sec

Weird Science

If a pinhead-size piece of the Sun were placed on Earth, one would have to stand as far as 90 miles away to be safe.

Spot the

0 8

differences!

☐
☐
☐
☐
☐
☐
☐
☐

EXTREME

ANSWERS ON PAGE 142

Time yourself

__ __ : __ __
min   sec

Taking Care of Business

"There are no secrets to success. It is the result of preparation, hard work, learning from failure." – Colin Powell

Spot the
0 9
differences!

☐
☐
☐
☐
☐
☐
☐
☐
☐

EXTREME

ANSWERS ON PAGE 142

Time yourself

__ __ : __ __
min   sec

Aloha!

See if you can spot all the changes made to the tropical garden.

Spot the
0 7
differences!

☐
☐
☐
☐
☐
☐
☐

EXTREME

ANSWERS ON PAGE 143

Time yourself

__ __ : __ __
min   sec

Diver's Paradise

Florida's coral reefs came into existence 5,000 to 7,000 years ago
when sea levels rose following the last Ice Age.

Spot the
0 9
differences!

☐
☐
☐
☐
☐
☐
☐
☐
☐

EXTREME

ANSWERS ON PAGE 143

Time yourself

__ __ : __ __
min   sec

Green Green Grass Of Home

"There is no place more delightful than one's own fireside."
– Cicero

Spot the
08
differences!

EXTREME

ANSWERS ON PAGE 143

Time yourself

__ __ : __ __
min   sec

Just Go For It!

"Only those who will risk going too far can possibly find out how far one can go." – T.S. Eliot

EXTREME

Spot the

0|7

differences!

☐
☐
☐
☐
☐
☐
☐

EXTREME 🔍🔍🔍🔍🔍

ANSWERS ON PAGE 143

Time yourself

__ __ : __ __

min   sec

Lost Your Marbles?

Did you know that marbles were originally made out of alabaster?

Spot the
0 8
differences!

☐
☐
☐
☐
☐
☐
☐
☐

EXTREME

ANSWERS ON PAGE 143

Time yourself

_ _ : _ _
min   sec

Go SeaBiscuit…Go

Did you know that the lightest jockey on record weighed in at 49 lb!

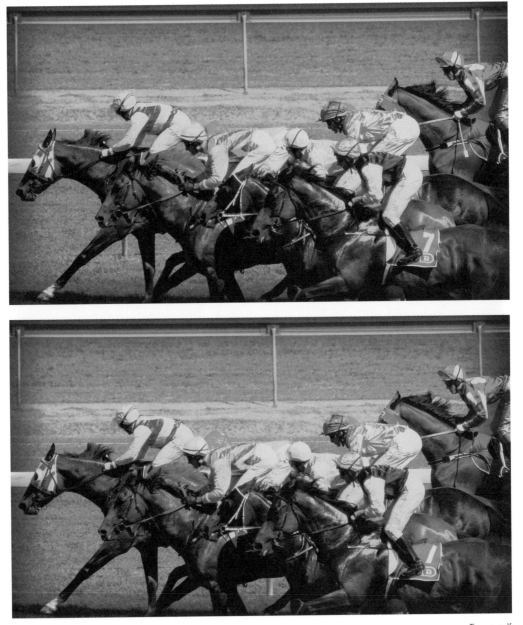

Spot the

10

differences!

☐
☐
☐
☐
☐
☐
☐
☐
☐
☐

EXTREME

ANSWERS ON PAGE 143

Time yourself

__ __ : __ __
min   sec

Sail Away!

The longest pleasure pier in the world is at Southend-on-Sea, Essex.
It extends 7,080 feet into the Thames estuary in the UK.

Spot the
0 8
differences!

☐
☐
☐
☐
☐
☐
☐
☐

EXTREME

ANSWERS ON PAGE 144

Time yourself

__ __ : __ __
min   sec

Need A Hand?

The Library of Congress, Washington DC, USA contains 28 million books and has 532 miles of shelving.

Spot the
1 0
differences!

EXTREME

ANSWERS ON PAGE 144

Time yourself

___ : ___
min   sec

Every Baker's Pride!

Before you devour all the yummy bread, see if you can spot the changes.

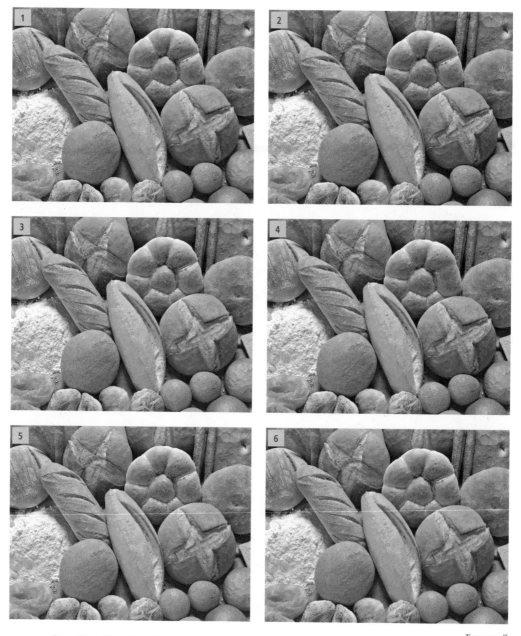

EXTREME

ANSWERS ON PAGE 144

Time yourself

__ __ : __ __
min   sec

Little Genius

The word "pencil" comes from the Latin word "pencillus"
which means little tail.

EXTREME

ANSWERS ON PAGE 144

Time yourself

__ : __
min   sec

Page 09:

Page 10:

Page 11:

Page 12:

Page 13:

Page 15:

Page 16:

Page 17:

Page 18:

Page 19:

Page 20:

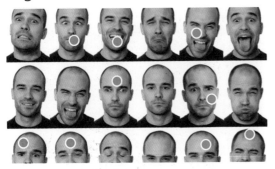

Page 21:

Page 22:

Page 23:

Page 25:

Page 26:

Page 27:

Page 28:

Page 29:

Page 33:

Page 34:

Page 35:

Page 36:

Page 37:

Page 38:

Page 39:

Page 40:

Page 41:

Page 42:

Page 43:

Page 45:

Page 46:

Page 47:

Page 48:

Page 49:

Page 50:

Page 51:

Page 52:

Page 53:

Page 57:

Page 58:

Page 59:

Page 60:

Page 61:

Page 62:

Page 63:

Page 64:

Page 65:

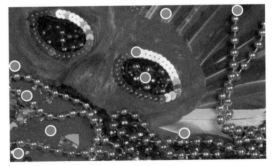

Page 67:

Page 68:

Page 69:

Page 70:

Page 71:

Page 73:

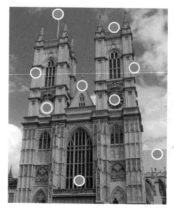

Page 74:

Page 75:

Page 76:

Page 77:

Page 78:

Page 79:

Page 83:

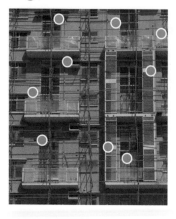

Page 84:

Page 85:

Page 86:

Page 87:

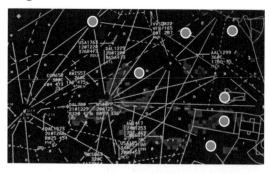

Page 88:

Page 89:

Page 90:

Page 91:

Page 92:

Page 93:

Page 95:

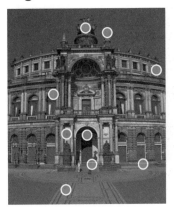

Page 96:

Page 97:

Page 98:

Page 99:

Page 100:

Page 101:

Page 102:

Page 103:

Page 107:

Page 108:

Page 109:

Page 110:

Page 111:

Page 112:

Page 113:

Page 114:

Page 115:

Page 116:

Page 117:

Page 118:

Page 119:

Page 121:

Page 122:

Page 123:

Page 124:

Page 125:

Page 126:

Page 127: